Amazing Omelet Recipes

A Complete Cookbook of Down-Home Dish Ideas!

BY: Allie Allen

COOK & ENJOY

Copyright 2020 Allie Allen

Copyright Notes

This book is written as an informational tool. While the author has taken every precaution to ensure the accuracy of the information provided therein, the reader is warned that they assume all risk when following the content. The author will not be held responsible for any damages that may occur as a result of the readers' actions.

The author does not give permission to reproduce this book in any form, including but not limited to: print, social media posts, electronic copies or photocopies, unless permission is expressly given in writing.

Table of Contents

Introduction 6

Breakfast was the original meal where omelets were most commonly served. They are still eaten often for breakfast. Here are some of the best... 8

   1 – Classic Bacon Omelet.. 9

   2 – Basic Breakfast Omelet... 12

   3 – Traditional French Omelet 14

   4 – Bacon & Mushroom Omelet 16

   5 – Microwave Breakfast Omelet 19

Omelets aren't just for breakfast anymore! They can make tasty lunch and dinner dishes, too. Here are some of the best.. 21

   6 – Fried Rice & Chicken Omelet 22

   7 – Kale & Avocado Omelet.. 24

   8 – Green Pepper & Tomato Omelet 26

   9 – Western Omelet 28

   10 – Mushroom & Herbs Omelet 31

   11 – Greek Egg White Omelet 34

12 – Southwestern Omelet 36

13 – Chicken & Spinach Omelet 38

14 – Cream Cheese & Asparagus Omelet 40

15 – Mushroom & Onions Omelet 42

16 – Ham & Feta Cheese Omelet 44

17 – Garden Vegetable Omelet 47

18 – Goat Cheese & Vegetable Omelet 50

19 – Cheesesteak Omelet 53

20 – Cheese 'n Chive Omelet 56

21 – Ham & Veggie Omelet 58

22 – Broccoli and Cheese Omelet 61

23 – Pepperoni Pizza Omelet 63

24 – Corn & Salsa Omelet 66

25 – Asparagus & Bacon Omelet 68

Omelets make wonderful bases for some very tempting dessert treats, too! Here are a few special dessert omelets. 70

26 – Blackberry Jam Omelet 71

27 – Puffy Strawberry Dessert Omelet 73

28 – Fruit & Vanilla Omelet 75

29 – Sweet Cinnamon Dessert Omelet.. 78

30 – Sweet Blueberry Omelet 80

Conclusion.. 82

About the Author.. 83

Author's Afterthoughts... 85

Introduction

How can you bring omelets into your own kitchen recipe collection?

Will your family enjoy the foray into omelets as much as they like other dishes?

Are the ingredients fairly easy to find, so you can make many types of omelets?

Your family will probably enjoy omelets for other meals, in addition to breakfast, the meal when they have probably had them before.

Meats make excellent additions to eggs for your omelets. You can use bacon, ham, cooked beef and even pepperoni for omelets served any time of day.

Veggie omelets are quite popular, too. From bell peppers and onions to mushrooms and tomatoes, and more, they make a healthy egg dish that is incredibly perfect for those who don't usually eat meat or simply want a change from recipes that include meats.

Dessert omelets are also popular. Many contain jam or berries, and the sweetest ones are usually made with sugar and cinnamon. Experiment with ingredients and enjoy the tastes!

Breakfast was the original meal where omelets were most commonly served. They are still eaten often for breakfast. Here are some of the best…

1 – Classic Bacon Omelet

This breakfast is delicious and also fairly low in calories. Bacon is not normally known as diet food, of course, but turkey bacon makes it healthier.

Makes 1 Serving

Cooking + Prep Time: 20 minutes

Ingredients:

- 1 slice of bacon, turkey
- 1/4 cup of finely chopped onions
- 1 egg, large
- 2 egg whites from large eggs
- 1 tbsp. of milk, skim
- A dash of black pepper, ground
- 1/4 cup of Swiss cheese shreds

Instructions:

1. Heat non-stick skillet on med. heat. Add bacon to pan. Cook for five minutes while occasionally turning, till it becomes crisp.

2. When you can handle bacon, crumble into small-sized pieces. Set them aside in a bowl.

3. Reduce heat level to low. Using same skillet, cook onions for 8-10 minutes, while frequently stirring. Cook till caramel-colored and soft. Remove ovens from pan. Set aside.

4. In small-sized bowl, whisk milk, egg whites, eggs and pepper together till combined well.

5. Return heat to med-high. Coat skillet using non-stick spray. Pour egg mixture in pan. Coat entire bottom.

6. Cook egg mixture for two minutes, till bottom has formed cooked, firm skin.

7. Sprinkle bacon, cheese and onions on 1/2 of omelet.

8. Use a spatula to fold empty 1/2 of omelet over filled half, enclosing bacon, cheese and onions.

9. Cook for two minutes more, till omelet is cooked fully through. Slide onto plate and serve promptly.

2 – Basic Breakfast Omelet

This omelet is a perfect choice for those busy in the mornings during the week, but it's also customizable. On days when you have more time, you can play around with the ingredients for even more unique tastes.

Makes 1 Serving

Cooking + Prep Time: 10 minutes

Ingredients:

- 2 eggs, large
- 2 tbsp. of water, filtered
- 1 pinch of salt, kosher
- 1 pinch of pepper, ground
- Strawberries, fresh, sliced
- 1 tbsp. of vanilla extract

Instructions:

1. Whisk the water, eggs, kosher salt & ground pepper together.

2. Spray non-stick 8" skillet with natural cooking spray. Heat to med. Pour in the egg mixture. As the eggs are setting around the edges of skillet, push cooked eggs towards middle of the skillet. Swirl skillet so uncooked eggs will flow to open pan areas and cook.

3. When the eggs are nearly set on the surface, but are still moist-looking, cover 1/2 omelet with strawberries and vanilla. Fold unfilled half onto filled side.

4. Cook for one minute more. Slide omelet onto a plate and serve.

3 – Traditional French Omelet

This is a classic French omelet, but it's actually simple to master the recipe. Once you do, then you can change up ingredients to suit your individual tastes.

Makes 1 Serving

Cooking + Prep Time: 12 minutes

Ingredients:

- 2 tbsp. of oil, light olive
- 1 tbsp. of chopped, frozen butter, unsalted
- 3 eggs, large
- A dash of salt, sea
- A dash of pepper, freshly ground
- 2 tbsp. of shredded cheese, Gruyere
- 2 tsp. of finely chopped chives, fresh

Instructions:

1. Add oil to medium skillet. Heat on med-high.

2. Whisk eggs till frothy. Don't season yet. Stir 1/2 butter into eggs.

3. Add remainder of butter to skillet. Swirl till butter has melted and becomes bubbly and cloudy.

4. Pour eggs in heated skillet. As you are cooking, quickly move a dinner fork through them in small zig-zags and circles till eggs are about 80% cooked.

5. Smooth top egg surface with back of large kitchen spoon. Season eggs as desired.

6. Sprinkle cheese & herbs on eggs. Cover skillet.

7. Turn heat off. Let omelet keep cooking for two to three minutes more – a shorter time unless you want your eggs firmer.

8. Tilt skillet to side. Ease omelet from skillet onto plate. Roll into tube shape or fold and serve promptly.

4 – Bacon & Mushroom Omelet

Our family gets tired of cereals and grab and go muffin sandwiches for breakfast, so when I have time, I love to make them this omelet. It is flavorful and fresh and has a sauce that doubles as a great nacho dip.

Makes 2 Servings

Cooking + Prep Time: 1/2 hour

Ingredients:

- 3 chopped strips of bacon, lean
- 4 sliced medium mushrooms, fresh
- 4 eggs, large
- 1/4 tsp. of salt, kosher
- 2 tsp. of butter, unsalted

For the sauce

- 1 tbsp. of butter, unsalted
- 1 tbsp. of flour, all-purpose
- 1/2 cup of milk, 2%
- 3 tbsp. of cheddar cheese shreds
- 1 tsp. of Parmesan cheese shreds
- 1 tsp. of seasoning blend, taco
- Toppings, optional: shredded lettuce, sliced green onions, chopped tomatoes

Instructions:

1. In non-stick, small skillet, cook the mushrooms and bacon, occasionally stirring, on med. heat till mushrooms become tender and the bacon has become crisp. Remove and drain both on plate lined with paper towels. Discard any drippings.

2. In small-sized bowl, whisk the eggs and kosher salt.

3. In same skillet, heat 1 tsp. of butter on med-high. Pour in 1/2 egg mixture. Eggs should set promptly around edges.

4. As the eggs are setting, push cooked eggs toward middle of skillet, so uncooked eggs can flow to empty, hot areas of skillet to cook.

5. When eggs have thickened and there is not any egg liquid remaining, spoon 1/2 mushrooms mixture to one half of omelet. Fold in half. Slide on a plate.

6. Repeat steps 3-5 for second omelet.

7. To prepare sauce, melt 1 tbsp. of butter on med. heat in small pan. Add flour till smooth. Whisk in the milk gradually. Bring to boil while constantly stirring and cook for two to three minutes, till mixture thickens.

8. Stir in the cheeses and seasoning till cheese melts.

9. Serve omelets with sauce and toppings you prefer.

5 – Microwave Breakfast Omelet

This is a handy, 5-minute recipe that cooks an omelet in a cup in your microwave oven. It's quick and easy, so it can be a part of any mornings, even busy ones.

Makes 1 Serving

Cooking + Prep Time: 5 minutes

Ingredients:

- 1 tbsp. of milk, 2%
- 2 eggs, large
- 1 tbsp. of sour cream, light
- Salt, kosher, as desired
- Pepper, ground, as desired
- 2 tbsp. of cheese shreds, cheddar

Instructions:

1. Spray 8-oz. micro-wave-safe cup or mug with non-stick spray.

2. Drop milk, eggs & sour cream in cup. Mix till blended well. Season as desired.

3. Microwave egg mixture for 2 minutes in standard 800-1100 watt microwave, or till done. It will puff up near top of mug but will ease down when done. Sprinkle with cheese. Allow to stand for a minute and serve.

Omelets aren't just for breakfast anymore! They can make tasty lunch and dinner dishes, too. Here are some of the best...

6 – Fried Rice & Chicken Omelet

This is a clever recipe that uses up leftover cooked rice and chicken. (They don't HAVE to be leftovers, of course.) The omelet makes a great dinner.

Makes 1 Serving

Cooking + Prep Time: 1/2 hour

Ingredients:

- 1/4 cup of rice, cooked
- 1/4 cup of cubed chicken, cooked
- 1/4 cup of frozen/thawed vegetable blend, stir-fry type
- 1 tbsp. of teriyaki sauce, reduced sodium
- 1 tbsp. of butter, unsalted
- 3 eggs, large
- 3 tbsp. of water, filtered
- 1/8 tsp. of salt, kosher
- 1/8 tsp. of pepper, ground

Instructions:

1. Coat a non-stick, small skillet with non-stick spray. Sauté chicken, rice and veggies in the teriyaki sauce till heated fully through. Remove mixture from skillet. Set it aside.

2. In same small skillet, melt the butter on med-high.

3. Whisk water, eggs, kosher salt & ground pepper in a bowl. Add this mixture to the skillet.

4. As the eggs are setting, push cooked eggs toward middle of pan, so uncooked eggs can flow under them. When eggs have set, spoon the chicken mixture to one side and fold the other side of omelet over the filling. Slide the omelet on plate. Serve.

7 – Kale & Avocado Omelet

Actually, this is a wonderful choice for lunch or dinner. The kale is rich in fiber, and along with the avocado, it will allow you to feel full between meals.

Makes 1 Serving

Cooking + Prep Time: 12 minutes

Ingredients:

- 1 tsp. of milk, low-fat
- 2 eggs, large
- 2 pinches of kosher salt
- 2 tsp. of oil, olive
- 1 cup of kale, chopped
- 1 tbsp. of lime juice, fresh
- 1 tbsp. of chopped cilantro, fresh
- 1 tsp. of sunflower seeds, unsalted
- 1 pinch of red pepper, crushed
- 1/4 sliced avocado, fresh

Instructions:

1. Beat milk, eggs & kosher salt in small mixing bowl.

2. Next, heat 1 tsp. of oil in non-stick skillet on med. heat. Add egg mixture. Cook till bottom sets, one to two minutes. Flip over. Cook till omelet has set, 1/2 minute more. Then, transfer it to plate.

3. Toss kale with remainder of oil, cilantro, lime juice, sunflower seeds, red pepper and a pinch of kosher salt. Top omelet with kale salad & avocado and serve.

8 – Green Pepper & Tomato Omelet

Fresh tomatoes, green peppers and onions give this omelet a fresh taste from the garden. If you like, you can substitute other fresh veggies you may have in the house.

Makes 1 Serving

Cooking + Prep Time: 25 minutes

Ingredients:

- 1/3 cup of green pepper, chopped
- 2 tbsp. of onions, chopped
- 2 tsp. of oil, olive
- 1 tbsp. of butter, unsalted
- 3 eggs, large
- 3 tbsp. of water, filtered
- 1/8 tsp. of salt, kosher
- 1/8 tsp. of pepper, ground
- 1/3 cup of tomatoes, chopped

Instructions:

1. In small skillet, sauté the onions and green peppers in olive oil till tender. Remove them from the skillet. Set them aside.

2. In same skillet, add butter and melt on med-high.

3. Whisk water and eggs together. Add kosher salt and ground pepper. Add this mixture to the skillet.

4. As the eggs set at edges, push those eggs toward middle of skillet. This lets the uncooked eggs flow under and access the heated skillet so they cook, too.

5. When eggs have set, spoon the onions, green peppers and tomatoes onto one half of the omelet. Fold the other half over the filling. Slide on a plate and serve.

9 – Western Omelet

This Western omelet is "styled" after the type of over-stuffed omelets that were once served in classic diners. The ham, cheese and bell peppers make a perfect lunch or supper.

Makes 2 Servings

Cooking + Prep Time: 20 minutes

Ingredients:

- 1 tbsp. of water, filtered
- 1/8 tsp. of salt, kosher
- 1/8 tsp. of pepper, freshly ground
- 4 eggs, large
- 1 tbsp. of oil, olive
- 1/2 cup of onions, 1" sliced
- 1/3 cup of bell peppers, red, 1" sliced
- 1/3 cup of bell pepper, green, 1" sliced
- 1/4 tsp. of chopped thyme, fresh
- 2 oz. of chopped ham, low sodium
- 1 oz. of Swiss cheese shreds

Instructions:

1. Combine the first four ingredients in med. bowl. Stir with whisk.

2. Heat non-stick, small skillet on med-high. Add 1 tsp. of oil and swirl, coating bottom.

3. Stir in the onions, ham, bell peppers and thyme. Sauté for four minutes, till veggies are tender-crisp. Remove from skillet. Set aside and clean the skillet.

4. Return skillet to med-high. Add 1 tsp. of oil and swirl, coating again. Add 1/2 egg mixture to skillet. Cook for one minute, till edges start setting. Lift the edge of your omelet and tilt the pan, allowing uncooked egg mixture to reach heated part of skillet bottom.

5. Repeat this procedure on other edges of the omelet. Cook for one minute, till center is barely set.

6. Evenly sprinkle 2 tbsp. of cheese on omelet. Add 1/2 veggie mixture atop cheese. Run a spatula around pan edges and under the omelet, loosening it from the pan. Fold it in half. Slide the omelet on a plate.

7. Repeat this procedure with the remainder of oil, then egg mixture, the cheese & veggie mixture. Serve.

10 – Mushroom & Herbs Omelet

The herbs won't overpower the other delicious flavors in this recipe. Rather, they will enhance them. It **Makes** a special dinner treat.

Makes 4 Servings

Cooking + Prep Time: 50 minutes

Ingredients:

- 1/4 cup of wine, white
- 1 lb. of sliced mushrooms, baby portobello
- 2 tbsp. of butter, unsalted
- 1 tsp. each of minced chives, parsley and tarragon, fresh
- 1/2 tsp. of chervil, dried
- 1/8 tsp. of salt, kosher
- 1/8 tsp. of pepper, ground

For the Asiago sauce

- 1 cup of milk, 2%
- 2 tbsp. of butter, unsalted
- 2 tbsp. of flour, all-purpose
- 1/4 cup of Asiago cheese, shredded
- 1/4 tsp. of salt, kosher

For the omelets

- 1/2 cup of water, filtered
- 8 eggs, large
- 4 tsp. of butter, unsalted

Instructions:

1. In large-sized skillet, sauté the mushrooms in unsalted butter till they are tender. Add the wine. Then, stir, loosening any browned bits from the pan. Add and stir in herbs, kosher salt & ground pepper. Remove from heat and set mixture aside.

2. To prepare sauce, in small pan, melt the butter. Stir while adding flour till you have a smooth mixture. Add milk gradually. Bring to boil. Then, stir while cooking for one to two minutes, till it thickens. Add and stir in the cheese and kosher salt and keep it warm.

3. In non-stick, small skillet, melt 1 tsp. of butter on med-high. Whisk the water and eggs till blended well. Add 2/3 cup of the egg mixture to heated skillet.

4. As the eggs are setting, push the cooked edge eggs toward middle, allowing the uncooked eggs to flow under them. When all eggs have set, spoon 1/2 cup of mushroom mixture on 1/2 omelet. Fold other 1/2 over the filling. Slide the omelet on plate and top using 1/4 cup of asiago sauce. Repeat with remainder of egg mixture. Serve.

11 – Greek Egg White Omelet

The egg whites lighten up this Greek omelet, but they don't have any negative effects on the overall taste. The spinach, juicy tomatoes, olives and feta cheese bring the Mediterranean taste home.

Makes 1 Servings

Cooking + Prep Time: 15 minutes

Ingredients:

- 4 eggs, large
- 1 tsp. of oil, olive
- Salt, kosher
- Pepper, ground
- 1/4 cup of tomatoes, cherry
- 1/4 cup of spinach, fresh
- 1/4 cup of cheese, feta
- 1/4 cup of olives, kalamata

Instructions:

1. Separate yolks from whites. Reserve yolks for other use.

2. Beat whites till a bit frothy. Add about 1/2 tsp. each of kosher salt & ground pepper.

3. Chop vegetables as you desire.

4. Heat oil in non-stick skillet on med. heat.

5. Lower heat level to low. Then pour egg whites in pan. Swirl till they fully coat bottom of pan.

6. Use spatula to pull eggs to middle of pan. Allow all eggs to reach exposed area of pan so all cook fully.

7. When egg is nearly set, add cheese and veggies to 1/2 omelet. Fold other 1/2 over filling. Cook for 30-60 more seconds till filling warms. Serve.

12 – Southwestern Omelet

In Southwestern communities, hearty dishes are popular. You'll love adding in flavors from the region to create this tasty recipe.

Makes 4 Servings

Cooking + Prep Time: 25 minutes

Ingredients:

- 1/2 cup of onion, chopped
- 1 minced pepper, jalapeno
- 1 tbsp. of oil, canola
- 6 lightly beaten eggs, large
- 6 cooked, crumbled strips of bacon
- 1 chopped tomato, small
- 1 x 1"-sliced avocado, ripe
- 1 cup of cheese shreds, Monterey Jack
- Salt, kosher & pepper, ground, as desired
- Optional: salsa, bottled

Instructions:

1. In large-sized skillet, sauté the jalapeno and onions till tender. Remove them and set mixture aside. Pour the eggs in same skillet and cover. Then, cook on low heat for three to four minutes.

2. Sprinkle eggs with onion/jalapeno mixture, 1/2 cup of cheese, avocadoes, tomatoes and bacon. Season as desired.

3. Fold 1/2 omelet over the filling. Cover pan. Cook for three to four minutes, till eggs have set. Sprinkle with the rest of the cheese. Serve along with salsa as desired.

13 – Chicken & Spinach Omelet

This omelet is filled with shredded chicken and healthy spinach. It comes together easily and quickly, and it has a creamy, rich texture, thanks to Gruyere cheese.

Makes 1 Serving

Cooking + Prep Time: 12 minutes

Ingredients:

- 4 beaten eggs, large
- Salt, kosher, as desired
- Pepper, ground, as desired
- 1 tsp. of oil, olive
- 1/3 cup of cooked chicken, shredded
- 2 tbsp. of Gruyere cheese shreds
- 2 tbsp. of spinach, chopped

Instructions:

1. Whisk eggs till whites and yolks are fully combined. Season as desired.

2. Heat 1 tsp. oil in non-stick skillet over high heat. Swirl oil around till it coats pan bottom.

3. Pour beaten eggs in skillet. Reduce heat level to low. Swirl eggs and coat pan bottom.

4. Pull egg from outside edge with spatula into middle of pan, exposing areas of pan where remaining egg can completely cook. Allow omelet to set for a couple minutes on low heat.

5. Warm chicken a bit in microwave. Add it, along with Gruyere shreds and spinach to 1/2 of omelet. Cook for 1/2 minute.

6. Fold other 1/2 of omelet over filling. Cook for 1/2 minute more, till cheese melts. Serve.

14 – Cream Cheese & Asparagus Omelet

When the asparagus in your garden is in season, you can use it in so many meals. This will be one of your favorites since it looks as good as it tastes.

Makes 2 Servings

Cooking + Prep Time: 25 minutes

Ingredients:

- 4 trimmed, 1"-cut asparagus spears, fresh
- 4 eggs, large
- 1/4 cup of sour cream, light
- 2 tsp. of dried onion, minced
- 1/4 tsp. of salt, kosher
- 1/4 tsp. of crushed pepper flakes, red
- 2 tsp. of butter, unsalted
- 2 oz. of cubed, softened cream cheese, reduced fat

Instructions:

1. Fill small pan 3/4 full using filtered water and bring it to boil. Add the asparagus. Leave pan uncovered and cook for two to four minutes, till tender-crisp. Remove from pan. Drop in ice water to stop heating process. Drain, then pat asparagus dry.

2. In small-sized bowl, whisk onions, sour cream, kosher salt & red pepper flakes together.

3. In non-stick, large skillet, heat the butter on med-high. Add egg mixture. Edges should set right away. As the eggs set, use a spatula to push cooked eggs toward middle of pan, so uncooked eggs can flow beneath them to cook.

4. When the eggs have all thickened, top 1/2 omelet with asparagus and cream cheese. Fold other 1/2 of omelet over fillings. Reduce the heat level to low. Cover the omelet and allow it to sit till cream cheese has melted, one to two minutes. Slice omelet in half to serve.

15 – Mushroom & Onions Omelet

This omelet has onions and mushrooms, making a great lunch or dinner. Cremini mushrooms have an earthy taste that works well, but other varieties will work, too.

Makes 1-2 Servings

Cooking + Prep Time: 20 minutes

Ingredients:

- 3 eggs, large
- Salt, kosher, as desired
- 2 tsp. + 1 tsp. of butter, unsalted
- 1/2 chopped onion, medium
- 4 oz. of cleaned, then trimmed & sliced mushrooms, cremini or your choice
- Optional: 2 tbsp. of cheddar cheese shreds; chives, freshly snipped

Instructions:

1. Crack eggs into medium bowl. Add a pinch of kosher salt. Whisk till beaten well, then set them aside.

2. Melt 2 tsp. butter in non-stick, large skillet on med. heat. Add onions. Sauté till translucent and soft, three to five minutes or so. Add mushrooms. Sauté till they are soft and have released their juices, three more minutes. Transfer onions with mushrooms to a bowl. Set it aside.

3. Wipe skillet out. Add 1 tsp. butter. Swirl to coat bottom of pan.

4. Pour beaten eggs into skillet. When edges start setting, run spatula around edges and push them towards center of pan. Tilt pan so uncooked egg can cook.

5. When egg surface is nearly set, top 1/2 of omelet with onions and mushrooms. Evenly sprinkle with cheese, as desired. Fold second 1/2 of omelet over filling. Flip stuffed omelet gently. Cook for a minute more, till cheese is melt-y and eggs have set fully.

6. Transfer omelet to plate. Use snipped chives to garnish, as desired. Serve promptly.

16 – Ham & Feta Cheese Omelet

I'll make a ham & cheese-based meal whenever I have the chance, and I make this omelet recipe a lot. It also offers bright tomatoes for color and taste.

Makes 2 Servings

Cooking + Prep Time: 25 minutes

Ingredients:

- 4 eggs, large
- 1 chopped onion, green
- 1 tbsp. of milk, 2%
- 1/4 tsp. of basil, dried
- 1/4 tsp. of oregano, dried
- A dash of garlic powder, mild
- A dash of salt, kosher
- A dash of pepper, ground
- 1 tbsp. of butter, unsalted
- 1/4 cup of feta cheese crumbles
- 3 slices of chopped deli ham
- 1 chopped tomato, plum
- 2 tsp. of vinaigrette, balsamic

Instructions:

1. In small-sized bowl, whisk the milk, green onions, eggs and seasonings, till blended well.

2. In non-stick, large skillet, heat the butter on med-high. Add egg mixture. The eggs around edges will immediately set.

3. As the eggs set, push the portions that have cooked toward middle, allowing uncooked part of eggs to flow beneath, so they can cook. When eggs have thickened, top 1/2 omelet with the ham and cheese.

4. Fold other 1/2 of omelet over filling and cut in two portions. Slide them onto two plates and top them with tomatoes. Drizzle with some vinaigrette and serve.

17 – Garden Vegetable Omelet

This omelet is a perfect choice for vegetarians, as it includes bell peppers and variations like pea pods, mushrooms, etc. You can also add garlic powder and onion powder if you like.

Makes 1 Serving

Cooking + Prep Time: 12 minutes

Ingredients:

- 4 beaten eggs, large
- 1 tbsp. of oil, olive
- Optional: 1/2 diced onion
- 1 chopped bell pepper, red or yellow
- 1 chopped bell pepper, green
- 1 tbsp. of butter, unsalted
- Salt, kosher, as desired
- Pepper, ground, as desired

Instructions:

1. Crack the eggs in small bowl. Use a fork to beat together well.

2. Heat non-stick skillet on med. heat. Add oil. Add onions, if including. Sauté for three to five minutes.

3. Add all bell peppers. Cook for one to two minutes, till peppers are a bit tender. Turn heat off.

4. Lift onions & peppers from skillet. Transfer to bowl with eggs. Combine fully.

5. Wipe skillet carefully with paper towels. Place on med. heat.

6. Add butter. Tilt pan to coat bottom. Pour in egg mixture. Season as desired.

7. Lift omelet edges when set so uncooked center sections can cook.

8. Allow omelet to continue cooking till bottom of eggs are solid but not yet browned at all.

9. Flip omelet and cook for one to two more minutes. Transfer to plate. Serve.

18 – Goat Cheese & Vegetable Omelet

Our family actually loves vegetables, even the younger children, so these omelets are a lunch or dinner treat we all enjoy. This recipe has a low prep time, so it's perfect, even on weeknights.

Makes 2 Servings

Cooking + Prep Time: 35 minutes

Ingredients:

- 4 eggs, large
- 1/4 cup of milk, whole
- 1/4 tsp. of salt, kosher
- 1/8 tsp. of pepper, ground
- 4 tsp. of oil, olive
- 1 cup of zucchini, sliced thinly
- 4 chopped small mushrooms, fresh
- 1/4 cup of green peppers, chopped finely
- 1 cup of baby spinach, fresh
- 2 thinly sliced onions, green
- 2 thinly sliced cloves of garlic
- 1/4 cup of goat cheese crumbles
- Optional: extra green onions, thinly sliced

Instructions:

1. First, in small-sized bowl, whisk the milk, eggs, kosher salt & ground pepper. In non-stick, large skillet, heat 2 tsp. of oil on med-high. Add the mushrooms, green peppers and zucchini. Then, stir while cooking for three to five minutes, till tender.

2. Add the garlic, spinach and green onions. Stir while cooking for one to two more minutes, till garlic becomes tender and spinach wilts. Transfer the vegetable mixture into small bowl.

3. Next, in the same skillet, heat the remainder of oil. Pour egg mixture in. The edges should set right away.

4. As eggs are setting, push the cooked eggs toward middle of skillet, so the uncooked eggs can flow underneath and cook.

5. When the eggs have thickened, spoon the veggie mixture on 1/2 of omelet. Sprinkle cheese on top. Fold bare half over filling. Cut omelet in half. Slide onto two plates. Sprinkle top with extra green onions, if using, and serve.

19 – Cheesesteak Omelet

Philly cheesesteaks, some of the best sandwiches you'll find, are faithfully recreated, plus eggs in this recipe. It's a savory, melty, delicious omelet.

Makes 1 Serving

Cooking + Prep Time: 25 minutes

Ingredients:

- 1/4 lb. of steak, shaved (you can substitute sliced chuck)
- 1/2 sliced onion, small
- A dash of Worcestershire sauce, low sodium
- 2-3 tbsp. of butter, unsalted
- 3 eggs, large
- 1/4 cup of cheese shreds, cheddar or mozzarella
- Salt, kosher, as desired
- Pepper, ground, as desired
- Optional: Sriracha sauce

Instructions:

1. Add kosher salt & ground pepper to shaved steak. Cook in sauté pan over high heat till browned. Flip. Finish cooking other side of steak.

2. Remove steak from pan. Add onions. Reduce heat level. Cook till browned and soft, five minutes or so. Add onions to steak. Add Worcestershire sauce.

3. Dice 1 tbsp. butter. Whisk eggs together till whites and yolks have barely combined. Stir in tiny butter cubes gently. Season as desired.

4. Add remainder of butter to large-sized frying pan. Allow it to heat over med-high till it begins to foam and nearly turns brown.

5. Add egg mixture to heated pan. Gently swirl to mix eggs, without scraping pan bottom. Allow runny parts of egg to touch pan so they can cook.

6. Lift omelet edges with rubber spatula, allowing runny eggs to cook. Once omelet has set, add steak, shredded cheese and onions to middle of omelet. Immediately tilt pan so omelet rolls. This cooks omelet inside.

7. Continue tilting pan. Roll omelet on warm plate. Top with the Sriracha, if desired. Serve.

20 – Cheese 'n Chive Omelet

This omelet will fill you up for lunch or dinner. If you like, you can change out some of the ingredients to those you might like more.

Makes 2 Servings

Cooking + Prep Time: 20 minutes

Ingredients:

- 3 eggs, large
- 2 tbsp. of water, filtered
- 1/8 tsp. of salt, kosher
- A dash of pepper, ground
- 1 tbsp. of minced chives, fresh
- 1 tbsp. of butter, unsalted
- 1/4 – 1/2 cup of cheddar cheese shreds

Instructions:

1. In small bowl, whisk the water, eggs, kosher salt & ground pepper. Add and stir in the chives.

2. In non-stick, small skillet, heat the butter on med-high. Pour in the egg mixture. Edges should immediately set. As the eggs continue to set, push all cooked eggs toward middle of skillet, so the uncooked eggs can flow under them and cook.

3. When eggs have thickened, sprinkle cheese on 1/2 of omelet. Fold other 1/2 over cheese. Cut the omelet in halves. Slide them on plates and serve.

21 – Ham & Veggie Omelet

This omelet is a filling meal, piled high using ham, cheese, onions and bell peppers. It's easy to customize, too, according to your likes.

Makes 2 Servings

Cooking + Prep Time: 25 minutes

Ingredients:

- 1 tsp. of oil, canola
- 1/4 cup of diced onions, white
- 1/3 cup of diced bell peppers, green
- 1/3 cup of diced ham, thick-cut, or Canadian bacon
- Salt, kosher, as desired
- Pepper, ground, as desired
- 1 tbsp. of butter, unsalted
- 4 beaten eggs, large
- 1/2 cup of grated cheese, cheddar

Instructions:

1. Heat oil in non-stick, 12" skillet on med-high. Add ham, onions and bell peppers. Sauté for two minutes or so, till browned lightly. Vegetables should be tender-crisp. Season as desired.

2. Remove ham and vegetables to plate. Use dry paper towels to wipe out skillet carefully.

3. Reduce heat level to med-low. Add butter to skillet. After it melts, tilt pan and swirl to coat bottom. Add eggs.

4. As eggs set around edges, use spatula to lift edges so liquid egg can run to middle of skillet and cook.

5. Season omelet as desired. Top with cheese all over. Cover skillet for a minute, till cheese melts. Turn heat off.

6. Add back ham and cooked vegetables in middle of omelet. Use spatula around edges to loosen. Be careful not to tear the omelet.

7. Fold 1/2 of omelet over filling. Overlap with other side, creating a packet. Slide onto plate. Serve promptly with salsa or hot sauce, if you like.

22 – Broccoli and Cheese Omelet

This special recipe came from an Italian friend who served it for lunch or dinner and sometimes ate it on Italian bread. Actually, it's a great way to use up broccoli.

Makes 4 Servings

Cooking + Prep Time: 35 minutes

Ingredients:

- 6 eggs, large
- 2 & 1/2 cups of broccoli florets, fresh
- 1/4 cup of milk, 2%
- 1/2 tsp. of salt, kosher
- 1/4 tsp. of pepper, ground
- 1/3 cup of Romano cheese, grated
- 1/3 cup of Greek olives, sliced and pitted
- 1 tbsp. of oil, olive
- To garnish: minced parsley and Romano cheese, shaved

Instructions:

1. Preheat your oven broiler.

2. In large sized pan, place a steamer basket over an inch of tap water. Place the broccoli in the basket. Bring the water to boil. Reduce heat level to a simmer. Then, cover and steam for four to six minutes, till broccoli is tender-crisp.

3. In large-sized bowl, whisk the milk, eggs, kosher salt and ground pepper together. Add and stir in the cooked broccoli, then olives and grated cheese.

4. In oven-proof, 10" skillet, heat oil on med. heat. Pour in the egg mixture. Leave uncovered and cook for four to six minutes, till eggs have nearly set.

5. Broil three to four inches from heat for two to four minutes, till eggs set completely. Allow them to stand for five minutes. Slice in wedges. Sprinkle with parsley and shaved cheese and serve.

23 – Pepperoni Pizza Omelet

Since everybody loves pizza, why not cross it with an omelet for a tasty lunch or dinner? Omelet lovers will find themselves gobbling up this terrific meal treat, too.

Makes 1 Serving

Cooking + Prep Time: 12 minutes

Ingredients:

- 4 beaten eggs, large
- Salt, kosher, as desired
- Pepper, ground, as desired
- 1/2 tsp. of oil, olive
- 2 tbsp. of warmed tomato sauce, no salt added
- 2 tbsp. of mozzarella cheese shreds
- 1/4 cup of chopped pepperoni
- For garnishing: chopped parsley and/or chopped basil

Instructions:

1. Use a whisk to beat eggs till whites and yolks are combined completely. Season as desired.

2. Heat oil in non-stick skillet on med-low. Swirl oil and coat pan completely. Reduce heat to low.

3. Add eggs to skillet. Swirl quickly and cover bottom of pan.

4. Move eggs with spatula from edges to middle of skillet, exposing pan bottom so remainder of eggs can cook fully. Leave them undisturbed and let them cook till omelet is nearly set.

5. When omelet has almost set, slowly spoon tomato sauce on 1/2. Cover sauce with cheese shreds and pepperoni. Cook for 1/2 minute more, till bottom is nearly browned.

6. Fold bare 1/2 of omelet over filling. Cook for 1-2 minutes till cheese melts and omelet is heated fully through.

7. Top with chopped parsley and/or basil, as desired. Serve.

24 – Corn & Salsa Omelet

This omelet tastes great, whether you use home-grown or frozen corn and salsa made at home or from a jar. Customize it by sprinkling on meat, peppers, mushrooms and onions if you like.

Makes 4 Servings

Cooking + Prep Time: 1/2 hour

Ingredients:

- 10 eggs, large
- 2 tbsp. of water, filtered
- 1/4 tsp. of salt, kosher
- 1/4 tsp. of pepper, ground
- 2 tsp. + 2 tbsp. of butter, unsalted
- 1 cup of corn, frozen & thawed or fresh
- 1/2 cup of cheddar cheese shreds
- Salsa, bottled

Instructions:

1. In small mixing bowl, whisk water, eggs, kosher salt & ground pepper till blended well.

2. In non-stick, large skillet, heat 2 tsp. of butter on med. heat. Add the corn. Stir for one to two minutes, till corn is tender. Remove it from the pan.

3. In the same skillet, heat 1 tbsp. butter on med-high. Pour in 1/2 egg mixture. Edges should set readily. As the eggs are setting, push the cooked eggs toward middle of pan. The other eggs will run underneath them and cook.

4. When all eggs are cooked and thickened, spoon 1/2 corn on 1/2 of omelet. Sprinkle using 1/4 cup of cheese shreds. Fold empty side over filling. Cut into halves. Slide halves on plates.

5. Repeat with remainder of butter, then egg mixture, then filling. Serve with the salsa, as desired.

25 – Asparagus & Bacon Omelet

Bacon and tender asparagus create a wonderful match when you make this easy spring omelet. Thin stalks of asparagus are best, as they have a bite to them, but also cook quickly.

Makes 1 Serving

Cooking + Prep Time: 1/2 hour

Ingredients:

- 10 oz. of 1/3"-cut asparagus
- 6 eggs, large
- 1/3 cup of Parmesan cheese, grated
- 1/2 tsp. of salt, kosher
- 1/4 tsp. of pepper, ground
- 4 slices of 1/2"-cut pieces bacon
- 4 white parts of green onions, sliced thinly

Instructions:

1. Steam the asparagus till crisp-tender, five minutes or so. Drain well.

2. Whisk the eggs with grated Parmesan, kosher salt & ground pepper in large mixing bowl, blending well.

3. Sauté pieces of bacon in non-stick, large skillet on med-high till golden brown in color, three minutes. Add green onions. Sauté till translucent, three minutes. Add the cooked asparagus and sauté till it has heated fully through.

4. Lower heat level to med. Spread asparagus and bacon mixture in one layer in the skillet. Pour the egg mixture slowly over the asparagus.

5. Cook till eggs have set softly. Tilt skillet and run spatula gently around the edges, moving cooked eggs to middle of pan so the remainder can flow under them and cook, four minutes or so. Slide omelet on plate and fold in half. Garnish as desired and serve.

Omelets make wonderful bases for some very tempting dessert treats, too! Here are a few special dessert omelets.

26 – Blackberry Jam Omelet

This sweet and fluffy omelet harkens back to the early days of omelets when jam and berries were used as often as cheese for filling. You'll enjoy the taste if you like toast and jam.

Makes 4 Servings

Cooking + Prep Time: 15 minutes

Ingredients:

- 4 separated eggs, large
- 1 tbsp. of sugar, granulated
- 2 tbsp. of cream, thick + extra for serving, as desired
- 3/4 ounce of butter, unsalted
- 3 tbsp. of jam, blackberry
- For dusting: 2 tbsp. of sugar, powdered

Instructions:

1. Preheat a grill for high heat.

2. Beat the cream, egg yolks and sugar in mixing bowl till pale.

3. In separate bowl, beat the egg whites till they are soft. Fold gently into yolk mixture.

4. Melt butter in medium skillet. When it starts foaming, add egg mixture. Then, cook on low for one to two minutes till base sets and eggs start coming away from pan sides.

5. Place under grill, 4 inches from heat. Cook for two to three minutes, till barely set.

6. Heat jam in pan on low heat. Spread over omelet. Fold omelet in halves. Dust with powdered sugar. Slice in four wedges. Serve with thick cream, if desired.

27 – Puffy Strawberry Dessert Omelet

This is a wonderful sweet treat of an omelet. It takes a bit of time to prepare, but it is SO worth it.

Makes 4 Servings

Cooking + Prep Time: 35 minutes

Ingredients:

- 6 separated eggs, large
- 1/2 tsp. of salt, kosher
- 1/4 cup of sugar, granulated
- 2 tbsp. of flour, all-purpose
- 2 tsp. of lemon zest, grated
- 1 tsp. of vanilla extract, pure
- 2 tbsp. of butter, unsalted
- 1 pint of sliced, sweetened strawberries, fresh
- Whipped cream, as desired

Instructions:

1. In medium bowl, beat kosher salt with egg whites till they form stiff peaks. Set the bowl aside.

2. In separate bowl, beat egg yolks, flour, sugar, vanilla and lemon zest till smooth. Then fold in the egg whites.

3. In an oven-proof, 10" skillet, melt the butter on med-low. Add the egg mixture. Allow to cook without any stirring for six to seven minutes, till bottom is a golden brown color. Remove pan from the heat.

4. Broil four inches from heat for a minute, till top turns golden. Fold the omelet in halves. Transfer to plates. Top with fresh strawberries, then whipped cream and serve.

28 – Fruit & Vanilla Omelet

This sweet dessert omelet can be filled with your choice of mixed fruits, then folded and dusted with powdered sugar. The taste is fresh and so delicious!

Makes 2 Servings

Cooking + Prep Time: 15 minutes

Ingredients:

- 4 separated eggs, large
- 1/2 cup of sugar, granulated
- 1 white from large egg
- 1 tbsp. of water, filtered
- 3 tbsp. of fruit, mixed, your choice
- To fry: butter, unsalted
- 1 tbsp. of sugar, powdered
- 1 cup of whipping cream
- 1 tsp. of vanilla extract, pure

Instructions:

1. Preheat the oven to 350F.

2. Whip the cream, then add vanilla extract and granulated sugar. Set aside.

3. Place oven-proof skillet over med. heat on stove top burner.

4. Next, beat the egg whites till they form stiff peaks.

5. Whisk the sugar into egg yolks till pale and thick.

6. Fold egg whites into the yolk mixture. Don't allow the whites to deflate.

7. Pour half of mixture into skillet. Swirl to smooth the top.

8. Next, cook for 1/2 minute to 1 minute. Place in 350F oven for two to three minutes, till golden and puffed. Set aside.

9. Repeat steps to make second omelet.

10. Pour fruits over 1/2 omelets. Cover with whipped cream.

11. Fold omelets over. Use powdered sugar to dust, then serve.

29 – Sweet Cinnamon Dessert Omelet

This cinnamon omelet is among my family's favorite a simple dessert. It's like cinnamon crepes but easier for you to make.

Makes 1 Serving

Cooking + Prep Time: 20 minutes

Ingredients:

- 2 to 3 tbsp. of milk, 2% or whole
- 2 eggs, large
- 2 to 3 tsp. of syrup, maple
- 1/2 tsp. of cinnamon, ground
- 1 cup of mixed berries, frozen
- 3/4 to 1/2 cup of Greek yogurt
- To cook: oil, olive
- To top: handful of granola

Instructions:

1. Place the berries in small pan. Add 1/4 cup filtered water. Cook while occasionally stirring on stove top burner over low heat till thickened and warm. Set berries aside.

2. Whisk together milk, eggs, syrup and cinnamon. Heat non-stick, large skillet on med. heat. Add 1 tsp. oil.

3. Pour egg mixture in. Cook till nearly set. Flip and allow to cook to one more minute.

4. Slide omelet on a plate. Spread 1/2 with yogurt and berries. Fold over 1/2 over filling. Sprinkle with granola if you like. Serve.

30 – Sweet Blueberry Omelet

This omelet is easy to make and not too different in flavor from a popover or a souffle. It's a tasty and simple dessert.

Makes 1 Serving

Cooking + Prep Time: 25 minutes

Ingredients:

- 2/3 cup of blueberries, frozen or fresh
- 1/2 tbsp. of sugar or honey
- 2 eggs, large
- 2 tsp. + a pinch of sugar, granulated
- 1/2 tsp. of vanilla extract, pure
- 1/2 tbsp. of butter, unsalted

Instructions:

1. Combine berries with sugar or honey in small pan on med-low. Bring to very low boil. Reduce heat level to low. Cover pan and simmer till the mixture is saucy, eight to 10 minutes.

2. Separate one egg. Put white in bowl by itself. Combine yolk with the whole egg in small bowl. Add just a pinch of granulated sugar to egg white. Whisk till soft peaks form.

3. Whisk vanilla and 2 tsp. sugar into egg + yolk mixture till combined fully. Fold whipped white gently into other egg mixture.

4. In non-stick, medium skillet, heat butter on med. to med-low heat till it melts and starts foaming. Add eggs. Cook without stirring till eggs set well and are about 75% cooked through. Flip omelet with spatula. Allow to cook for a minute more. Top with 1-2 spoons of berry mixture. Fold omelet over filling and transfer to plate. Serve.

Conclusion

This omelet cookbook has shown you…

How to use different ingredients to affect unique, sweet & savory tastes in various omelets.

How can you include omelet recipes in your home repertoire?

You can…

- Make traditional French omelets and bacon & mushroom omelets, which you may have heard of before. They are undoubtedly just as tasty as they sound.
- Cook hearty meat omelets, using sausage, beef, bacon, ham and more. Find these ingredients in meat or frozen food sections of your local grocery store.
- Enjoy making delectable poultry omelets, including chicken or turkey. Protein is a mainstay of this omelet type, and there are SO many ways to make them great.
- Make omelets using vegetables like bell peppers, onions, tomatoes and more. There is something about them that rounds out the taste of the eggs.
- Make all kinds of desserts like sugary cinnamon omelets and fresh berry omelets, which will surely tempt anyone with a sweet tooth.

Enjoy these delectable recipes with your family and friends!

About the Author

Allie Allen developed her passion for the culinary arts at the tender age of five when she would help her mother cook for their large family of 8. Even back then, her family knew this would be more than a hobby for the young Allie and when she graduated from high school, she applied to cooking school in London. It had always been a dream of the young chef to study with some of Europe's best and she made it happen by attending the Chef Academy of London.

After graduation, Allie decided to bring her skills back to North America and open up her own restaurant. After 10 successful years as head chef and owner, she decided to sell her business and pursue other career avenues. This monumental decision led Allie to her true calling, teaching. She also started to write e-books for her students to study at home for practice. She is now the proud author of several e-books and gives private and semi-private cooking lessons to a range of students at all levels of experience.

Stay tuned for more from this dynamic chef and teacher when she releases more informative e-books on cooking and baking in the near future. Her work is infused with stores and anecdotes you will love!

Author's Afterthoughts

I can't tell you how grateful I am that you decided to read my book. My most heartfelt thanks that you took time out of your life to choose my work and I hope you find benefit within these pages.

There are so many books available today that offer similar content so that makes it even more humbling that you decided to buying mine.

Tell me what you thought! I am eager to hear your opinion and ideas on what you read as are others who are looking for a good book to buy. Leave a review on Amazon.com so others can benefit from your wisdom!

With much thanks,

Allie Allen

Printed in Great Britain
by Amazon